THE CHRISTIAN MOTHER

THE CHRISTIAN MOTHER

MARIA ELIZA HOARE,
EDWARD HOARE

ISBN: 978-93-93693-06-8

Published: 1876

LECTOR HOUSE LLP
E-MAIL: lectorpublishing@gmail.com

THE CHRISTIAN MOTHER:

OR,
NOTES FOR MOTHERS' MEETINGS.

BY THE

LATE MRS E. HOARE

WITH PREFACE BY
EDWARD HOARE

SECOND EDITION.

1876

PREFACE TO SECOND EDITION.

The following Notes were prepared and published some years ago, by one who has since realised in Heaven the unspeakable value of those precious truths which she most diligently taught on earth. The little book has been for a long time out of print, but it appears so calculated to be useful in the Lord's service that I have thought it well to publish another edition. It was said of Abel, 'He being dead yet speaketh.' May the admirable mother by whom these notes were prepared so speak in these pages to those who know a mother's care, that they may be assisted to enjoy the full experience of a mother's joy!

E. HOARE.

Tunbridge Wells,
April, 1876.

PREFACE.

THE following notes have been used by the writer in conducting Mothers' Meetings amongst the poorer classes, and it has been suggested that they may be useful to other ladies engaged in a similar work.

With this view, she has ventured to publish them in the present concise form.

It will be seen that they are merely skeletons, and will require to be filled up by each person who makes use of them. Thus it will be necessary to *turn to the texts referred to*, and to enlarge on each head as familiarly as possible, illustrating it by simple, and telling facts.

If this is done, and the subjects well studied, it will often be found, that, although each subject has been generally compressed into one chapter, it is better to take one, two, or three heads, as affording sufficient matter for the conversation of a single evening, rather than too hastily to go over the whole section.

It will be a cause for thankfulness, if these short notes may be the means of leading any mothers to search the Scriptures more diligently with reference to their own especial duties.

Whether rich or poor—educated or uneducated—mothers all need, in the great essentials, the *same* help, the *same* warnings, the *same* encouragements. They want to be comforted, both in duty and trial, by the *same* word of promise, and to 'go boldly to the *same* throne of grace to obtain mercy, and find grace to help in time of need.' It is earnestly desired that the study of the following pages, which are, in fact, only a compilation of Scripture, may be the means of leading many to listen more closely to *His* voice, who knows so well the mother's heart, the mother's sins, the mother's sorrows, and the mother's need.

M. E. H.

TUNBRIDGE WELLS,
December, 1862.

CONTENTS

I.

IMPORTANCE OF CHILDREN.

'Take heed that ye despise not one of these little ones.' Matt. xviii. 10.

I. They are important to *Society*.

> Our future soldiers, sailors, servants, fathers, mothers, husbands, wives, &c., &c.

II. Important to *yourselves*.

> The babe—the child—the young man—the young woman.

> A gift (Gen. xxxiii. 5; xlviii. 9) which must prove either your crown (Prov. xvii. 6; Ps. cxxvii. 3) or your bitterness. Prov. xvii. 25; Gen. xlii. 38.

III. Important to *themselves*.

> That child must live for ever.

> A living soul committed to your care.

> That child must stand before the judgment-seat of Christ. Rev. xx. 12.

IV. Important in the sight of *their Father who is in heaven*.

> So important—that for them He gave His only Son to shed His blood.

> So important—that He especially calls, 'Suffer little children,' &c. Mark, x. 14.

> So important—that He gives His angels special charge over them. Matt. xviii. 10.

'Take heed then that ye despise not one of these little ones.'

No jewel so precious as the soul of your child, but how far more do parents often prize the casket containing it, than the gem itself!

No plant so needing watchful care and culture; Oh! neglect it not!

What have YOU done with your jewel, your plant?

II.

THE TEMPER OF THE WIFE, AND MOTHER.

I. What she should *not* be.

    1. Provoking. Eph. vi. 4. Prov. xv. 1. Gal. v. 26.

    2. Easily provoked. 1 Cor. xiii. 5. Jam. i. 19.

    3. Brawling. Prov. xxi. 9; xxv. 24.

    4. Contentious. Prov. xix. 13; xxi. 19; xxvii. 15.

II. What she *should* be.

    1. Gentle. 1 Thess. ii. 7. 1 Pet. iii. 4. Children are soon frightened by rough words, or rough treatment.

    2. Forbearing. Eph. iv. 2. Col. iii. 13. If *you* cannot bear with your children, who will?

    3. Patient. 1 Thess. v. 14. Eccles. vii. 8. A mother has need of great patience.

    4. Loving. Tit. ii. 4.

III. In your daily temper take Christ as your example.

'*Consider Him* who endured such contradiction of sinners against himself, lest ye be weary, and faint in your minds.' Heb. xii. 3.

III.

TRUTH.—PART I.

Importance of truth. Prov. xii. 19.

The liar's portion. Rev. xxi. 8; xxii. 15.

How can you enforce the necessity of truth, and the sin of lying upon your children?

I. You must enforce it by *example*.

    1. Never deceive them. The word passed must never be broken. Be careful, then, how you promise or threaten.

    2. Always adhere yourself closely to truth. In *little* things as well as *great*, in *deed* as well as *word*. What a warning is Rebecca (Gen. xxvii.) of the danger of the first downward step, and the baneful influence of a mother's evil example!

    3. Let them see that you cling closely to truth, even when it is to your own disadvantage. Ps. xv. 5, Prayer-book version.

    4. Never get out of a difficulty by an untruth.

II. To do this be ever—

Watchful. Ps. cxli. 3.

Prayerful. Ps. cxix. 29.

IV.

TRUTH.—PART II.

Last meeting we found that it is useless to enforce the necessity of truth, unless the mother is consistent in her *example*. Besides this:

II. Enforce it by instruction and by precept.

Tell—how God hates lying. Prov. vi. 16, 17; xii. 22.

Tell—histories from Scripture to show how God hates it. Satan, Gen. iii. 4. Gehazi, 2 Kings, v. 25. Ananias, Acts, v. 1–11.

Tell—who is the father of lies. John, viii. 44.

Tell—the consequences of lying. Ps. v. 6; lv. 23. Rev. xxi. 8.

III. Avoid severity.

Children are often frightened into deceit by fear of their parents' severity.

IV. Do not put temptations to lie in a child's way.

Do not encourage them to conceal anything from their father, schoolmaster, master, or mistress, if in service.

V. Correct for a lie.

It is a false love which dispenses with a needful chastisement. Prov. xiii. 24; xix. 18.

But always with prayer.

VI. Let the child see that you are grieved for his sin. That it gives you *sorrow*, not only causes *anger*. Ps. cxix. 158.

VII. Make it a subject of prayer with your child that the way of lying may be removed from him. Ps. cxix. 29. Prov. xxx. 8.

V.

THE EXCELLENT WOMAN.—AS A WIFE

Prov. xxxi.

As a Wife.

I. A wife *ought* to be a chief blessing; a good wife *is* so. Verse 10. Prov. xii. 4; xviii. 22; xix. 14.

II. Her husband can safely trust her. Ver. 11.

Money—children—sure of her affection—no secrets.

III. She does him good, and not evil all the days of her life. Verse 12.

Not like Eve. Gen. iii. 6.

Or Samson's wife. Enticing—coaxing—teazing—weeping—betraying. Judg. xiv. 16.

IV. She cares for his bodily wants. Verses 15, 23.

To do this must be a 'keeper at home.' Tit. ii. 5.

V. She submits if wills clash.

Not often the case in a happy home.

Yields cheerfully, not grudgingly, when in accordance with God's will. Col. iii. 18. Eph. v. 22.

VI. She endeavours to *win* her husband, does not try to *drive*. 1 Pet. iii. 1. 1 Cor. vii. 16.

Win to religion by displaying its beauty and brightness in your lives.

VII. She is a spiritual help to her husband. 1 Pet. iii. 7.

'Mutual help and comfort.' Marriage Service.

Not a hindrance. Luke, xiv. 20.

A wife has more opportunity than any one of seeing her husband's faults. Do not *talk* about them, but *pray* about them.

VI.

THE EXCELLENT WOMAN.—IN HER HOME

Prov. xxxi.

IN HER HOME.

I. She is diligent. Verses 13, 15, 18, 19, 22, 27. So 1 Tim. v. 10. Rom. xii. 8.

No gossiping; standing at doors; idling at neighbours.

Observe what is said of the diligent in the Book of Proverbs.

Maketh rich. Prov. x. 4.

Prospered (Prov. xii. 24, 27; xiii. 4; xxi. 5.) Sometimes worldly diligence leads to spiritual sloth. Let it not be so with you; but whilst you are 'not slothful in business,' be also 'fervent in spirit; serving the Lord.' Rom. xii. 11.

II. She is prudent. Verses 13, 14, 15.

Looks well to her goings. Prov. xiv. 15. Looks forward. Prov. xxii. 3; xxvii. 12. Enjoys a special blessing. Prov. xix. 14.

III. Overlooks her household. Verses 15, 21, 27.

Children, servants, if she has any.

Your household, of whomsoever it may consist, should share your blessings and privileges. Gen. xviii. 19. Lev. xvi. 17. Acts, xvi. 15.

Important to impress this upon your girls going to service. A *good* mistress *ought*, and *will*, look after them. No kindness in lax discipline. Look back to your own days of service. Who was the best mistress? 1 Tim. v. 14.

VII.

THE EXCELLENT WOMAN.—
IN HER CONVERSATION

Prov. xxxi.

IN HER CONVERSATION.

I. 'She openeth her mouth with *wisdom*,' verse 26.

    1. No foolish talking, or jesting. Job, xv. 3. Eph. v. 4.

    2. No chattering or gossip, which tends to penury. Prov. xiv. 23. Eccles. x. 11, 14.

    3. No deception. Prov. xxiv. 28; xx. 17.

II. 'In her tongue is the law of *kindness*,' verse 26.

    1. No tale-bearing or back-biting. Prov. xxv. 23; xxvi. 22. Ps. xv. 3.

    How mischievous. Prov. xxiv. 2.

    2. No flattering, like wicked woman. Prov. v. 3; vi. 24. Ps. v. 9.

III. How important to bridle the tongue. Jam. i. 26.

    There is often much wisdom in silence. Ps. xxxiv. 13. Prov. xvii. 28; xxix. 11.

    Let your conversation be as it becometh the gospel of Christ. Philip, i. 27. Ps. lxxvii. 12. Prov. xv. 4. 1 Pet. iii. 1. 2 Pet. iii. 11. Col. iii. 16.

    Make this your prayer. Ps. xix. 14; cxli. 3.

    Blessing promised. Ps. l. 23.

IV. Three good rules.

    1. So speak to your husband and children, that should these be your *last* words, you would not regret them.

    2. Never say anything of your neighbours you would dislike them to over-hear.

    3. In all your conversation, remember that the Lord is nigh, and hears each word.

VIII.

THE EXCELLENT WOMAN.—HER RELIGION

Prov. xxxi.

HER RELIGION.

I. The secret of her many excellencies here portrayed.

It did not consist in *beauty*. Verse 30. A pretty face often leads to ruin. Prov. xi. 22. Ezek. xxviii. 17.

Never make much of a child's beauty.

But it was this, she was a *religious* woman, actuated in all she did by the *fear of the Lord*. Verse 30.

The woman who fears the Lord.

1. Hates evil. Prov. viii. 13.

2. It is her moving principle, 'all the day long.' Prov. xxiii. 17.

3. She is happy, though poor. Prov. xv. 16.

4. It is her confidence and refuge in trial. Prov. xiv. 26.

5. It is *well* with her. Eccles. viii. 12.

II. She shows her love to Christ, by her love to His people. Verse 20.

Acts, ix. 36. Heb. xiii. 16.

You need not be *rich* to be *charitable*.

The poorest may give. 2 Cor. viii. 2.

God looks not at the size, or value of the gift, but the motive from which it springs. 2 Cor. viii. 12.

The widow's mite. Mark, xii. 42, 44.

The cup of cold water. Matt. x. 42; xxv. 35.

Nursing a sick neighbour. 1 Tim. v. 10.

IX.

THE EXCELLENT WOMAN.—HER REWARD

Prov. xxxi.

Her Reward.

I. Her children regard her with grateful love, and look back with thankfulness to her care and teaching. Verse 28. *e.g.* Timothy, 2 Tim. i. 5, and David, Ps. lxxxvi. 16; cxvi. 16.

II. Her husband confides in her, blesses her, honours her. Verse 28.

Eph. v. 25, 31. 1 Pet. iii. 7.

III. She reaps the fruit of her labours. Verse 31. Deut. iv. 40. Prov. xx. 7; xxii. 6; xxix. 17. 2 John, 4.

IV. She shall rejoice in time to come. Verse 25.

Not only in this world (Ps. cxviii. 15), but in the life to come.

In the future kingdom, will not her children, for whom she prayed and laboured, be to her, as St. Paul says his spiritual children will be to him, 'Her joy, her crown of rejoicing in the presence of our Lord Jesus Christ at His coming?' 1 Thess. ii. 19.

Let this cheer the faint-hearted and discouraged Christian mother; she sows perhaps now with bitter tears, but she shall 'reap in joy.'

X.

HOW TO SPEND SUNDAY.

'Remember the Sabbath Day to keep it holy.'

Mothers can effect much by domestic arrangement, and forethought.

I. Make Saturday a 'day of preparation.' 'Bake that which ye will bake to-day,' &c. Exod. xvi. 5, 23. Mark, xv. 42. Luke, xxiii. 54.

II. Endeavour to make the Sunday

    1. A *holy* day.

        Exod. xx. 10, 11. Deut. v. 12. Gen. ii. 3.

        To sanctify, signifies to set apart for a holy purpose. Thus in the New Testament the Sabbath is called 'the Lord's day.' Rev. i. 10, because a day devoted to His service.

    2. A *resting* day.

        Gen. ii. 3. Lev. xxiii. 3. Matt. xxiii. 56.

        Called 'the Sabbath of *rest.*' Lev. xxiii. 3. And 'the *rest* of the holy Sabbath.' Exod. xvi. 23. *Sabbath* signifies *rest*, and heaven, of which it is a type, is called, 'the keeping of a *Sabbath.*' Heb. iv. 9.

    3. A *happy* day.

        It is a *gift*, a *privilege*, not a task.

        Exod. xvi. 29. Isa. lviii. 13.

        Not esteemed to be such, unless God's service felt to be a *delight*. Others say, 'When will the Sabbath be gone?' Amos, viii. 5.

        Let there be no gloom in the home, but a cheerful sobriety.

    4. A *profitable* day.

        Though *rest*, not *idleness*. Children are always happiest when their minds are employed.

        To profit pay great attention to Public Worship, Deut. xxxi. 12, 13. Acts, xiii. 42; xvi. 13; xviii. 4. Heb. x. 25.

        Observe our Lord's example. Luke, iv. 16.

        The Sunday School is a great help to the poor mother.

Cultivate religious occupation. *e.g.* Find texts—repeat hymns—sing hymns, &c.

III. Observe the promise.

Isa. lvi. 2–7: lviii. 13, 14.

XI.

COMPANIONS.

I. Danger of bad companions.

One bad companion corrupts many. 'A little leaven leaveneth the whole lump.' 1 Cor. v. 6.

'Evil communications corrupt good manners.' 1 Cor. xv. 33.

Eph. v. 11. Prov. xxii. 24, 25.

You are warned in the Scriptures against making companions of:

1. Fools. Prov. xiii. 20.

2. Riotous. Prov. xxviii. 7.

3. Thieves. Isa. i. 23.

4. Depraved. Prov. xxix. 3. 1 Cor. v. 9.

5. Irreligious. 2 Thess. iii. 14. Jam. iv. 4.

If important for yourselves, doubly so for the young, unformed minds of your children.

II. Form good friendships.

'The friendship of the world is enmity with God.' Jam. iv. 4.

David chose his friends from those who feared God. Ps. cxix. 63. Heb. x. 33.

III. Observe three rules for the sake of your *children*, as well as *yourselves*.

1. Never harbour bad guests.

Lodgers—workpeople.

2. Never associate with the wicked, unless obliged to do so, or with a view to doing them good.

Even this needs caution.

3. Remember, 'A man is known by his friends.'

You and your children will be judged by the company you keep.

XII.

SLOTH.

I. The command to be diligent is plain. Rom. xii. 11. 2 Thess. iii. 10, 11.

II. See the miserable results of sloth.

    1. It leads to tattling. 1 Tim. v. 13.

    2. Decay. Eccles. x. 18.

    3. Difficulties. Prov. xv. 19.

    4. Waste. Prov. xviii. 9.

    5. Want. Prov. xx. 4; xxiv. 30, 34.

III. Contrast excellent woman (Prov. xxxi. 27) with the slothful person. Prov. xix. 24; xxiv. 30; x. 26.

IV. Learn a lesson from the ant for yourselves—for your children. Prov. vi. 6, &c.

    Give your children something to do.

    Remember, they must be *set to work*, though it is often more trouble to you to teach *them* to do it, than to do it *yourself*—yet persevere.

V. If not slothful in your temporal affairs, above all be not slothful concerning the salvation of your souls.

    Heb. vi. 11, 12. 2 Pet. i. 10.

XIII.

THE WATCHFUL MOTHER.

No eye should be so wakeful and watchful as a mother's.

I. Watch over your children *in infancy*.

> Exod. ii. 8. 1 Sam. i. 23.

> It is described as next to impossible for a woman to forget her sucking child. Isa. xlix. 15.

> A well-watched infancy, under God's blessing, avoids many future ills.

II. Watch over your children's *education*.

> Judg. xiii. 8.

> In every minute particular.

> Learning—clothing, &c. 1 Sam. ii. 19. Prov. xxxi. 21, 23.

> Contrast the dirty, unmended clothes of the poor, uncared-for child, with the clean and neatly mended garments of him whose childhood is guarded by the watchful eye of a mother.

III. Watch them in times of sickness and death.

> No eye so quick to discover a hidden ill.

> 2 Kings, iv. 19, 20. John, xix. 25.

IV. Above all watch over the precious soul.

> Never lose sight of the soul, in care for the body.

>> 1. *Watch*, as those that must give account. Heb. xiii. 17.

>> 2. *Watch*, to detect sin, and check its growth.

> Mark first sign of the plague spot.

>> 3. *Watch*, for opportunity to lead to Christ. Prov. xv. 23. Deut. vi. 6, 9. Mark, x. 13.

XIV.

THE HASTY MOTHER.

I. How common! Yet the Bible commands us not to be hasty. Eccles. vii. 9.

> A woman's ornament should be a meek, and quiet spirit (1 Pet. iii. 4), and a nurse is mentioned as being especially gentle to the little ones. 1 Thess. ii. 7.

II. Observe the angry woman,

> How foolish! Prov. xiv. 29; xxix. 20.
>
> How provoking! Prov. xv. 1.
>
> How wearing! Prov. xix. 13; xxvii. 15; xxi. 19.
>
> Drives the husband from his fireside.
>
> Sets an evil example to the children.
>
> Often does in her haste, what she heartily repents at leisure.

III. Therefore,

> 1. Put away anger. Eph. iv. 31.
>
>> Do not be *soon* angry. Prov. xiv. 17. Jam. i. 19.
>>
>> 'Meekness gives smooth answers to rough questions.'
>
> 2. Exercise self-control. Prov. xxv. 28; xvi. 32.
>
> 3. Teach it to your children.

III. Remember, a hasty temper is a *fault*, not a *misfortune*. Accustom yourself, and your children, to view it in its right light.

IV. Ask help from God to subdue it, for temper is hard to conquer, and meekness is a fruit of the Spirit. Gal. v. 22. Matt. v. 5.

> You *need help*, for there is much to provoke a wife, and mother.
>
> You *need help*, for you are very weak, but you can do all things through Christ who strengtheneth you. Phil. iv. 13.

XV.

THE WEARY MOTHER.

Many things below make a mother weary.

The blessing of *rest* is chiefly future.

Notice various things that often make mothers weary, and the remedy for them.

CAUSE.	REMEDY.
I. Weary with cares and sorrows— ready to exclaim, 'My burden is greater than I can bear.'	I. Do not carry your burden alone. Ps. lv. 22. 1 Pet. v. 7. Jer. xxxi. 25. *Hereafter* rest. Psa. xciv. 13. Isa. xiv. 3.
II. Weary with work.	II. Make more use of the rest of the Sabbath. Exod. xx. 8. Called 'Sabbath of *rest*.' Lev. xxiii. 3. *Hereafter*. Heb. iv. 9.
III. Weary with sickness. Job, vii. 3, 4. Isa. xxxviii. 12, 14. May be your own, your husband's, your children's. Wearisome nights of pain, or watching.	III. Comfort in time of sickness. Ps. xli. 3. Great alleviation in true spirit of submission. *Hereafter*. Isa. xxxiii. 24. Rev. xxi. 4.
IV. Weary of your sins. Ps. vi. 6; xxxviii. 4. Oft repented. Oft repeated.	IV. Come with your sins to Christ. Matt. xi. 28, 29. *Hereafter*. Rev. xxi. 27.

V. Weary with your children's sins.	V. Correct, and they shall give you rest. Prov. xxix. 17. Consider Christ, *lest ye be weary.* Heb. xii. 3.

Do you know where to go for rest? Jer. vi. 16. Or are you wandering hither and thither in vain, having forgotten your resting-place? Jer. l. 6. Remember, it is only to those who are in Christ that these promises of rest apply.

It is only His own sheep who can say, 'He maketh me to *lie down in green pastures.'*

To others there is no rest here, or hereafter, for, 'The wicked are like the troubled sea, when it *cannot rest.* . . . There is no peace, saith my God, to the wicked.' Isa. lvii. 20, 21.

XVI.

THE CARELESS MOTHER.

Isa. xxxii. 9–13.

Motherless children are often uncared for. No one '*naturally* cares for their state.' No child with a mother *ought* to be so. But too often mothers are careless about—

I. Their *minds*.

> No schooling—no teaching—no training—no Sunday School. Cares not whether in time, or too late—regular or truant, &c., &c.

II. Their *respectability*, and *associates*.

> Will take in bad lodgers, hire bad characters to help at the wash-tub because they can be had cheaper than the respectable, forgetting that 'a good name is rather to be chosen than great riches.' Prov. xxii. 1. Eccles. vii. 1.

> What guilty carelessness!

III. Their *happiness*.

> What misery here awaits a neglected child!

> What woe hereafter!

IV. Their *souls*.

> To a parent guilty of this carelessness, it is said, 'His blood will I require at thine hand.' Ezek. iii. 18, 19; xxxiii. 6.

> Have you ever lost a child, for whose soul you never cared? Pray Ps. li. 14.

> *This* arises from want of real religion.

> You do not know the immense value of a soul.

> Would you be thus careless of an earthly treasure? Would you not watch it—lock it up—guard it with a jealous eye? Your child's soul a treasure passing all price. Yet you allow Satan to steal it—bad companions to corrupt it—ruin it yourself by neglect. A thing neglected is ruined.

> Keep in view the judgment day.

> Will your child then say, 'No man cared for my soul'—'even my *mother* cared not that I perished!'

XVII.

THE CAREFUL MOTHER.

I. Careful in her *house*.

> No waste. Prov. xviii. 9. John, vi. 12.
>
> Yet not stingy. No needless expense—makes a little go a long way.

II. Careful over her *children*.

> Their *bodies*—health—clothes—future. 1 Tim. v. 8. 2 Cor. xii. 14.
>
> Provident Club. Penny Bank, &c.
>
> Their *minds*. Gives education suitable to their station. No fortune so good.
>
> What a disgrace in these days to a mother, if a child cannot read and write!
>
> Their *souls*. Above all, let not care for the body choke this. Mark, iv. 19.
>
> Lay up treasure in heaven. Matt. vi. 20.

III. Let not careful mother be *too full of care*.

> Not *overcharged*. Luke, xxi. 34; x. 41, 42.
>
> 'Live not in careful suspense.' Luke, xii. 29 (margin).
>
> Cast your care on One who can bear it. 1 Pet. v. 7. Phil. iv. 6. He will not despise it, *'for He careth for you.'*
>
> For the future, take this for your motto when over-pressed by cares and trials, 'The Lord will provide.' Gen. xxii, 14. Philip, iv. 19. Ps. xxiii. 1.

XVIII.

THE PATIENT MOTHER.

A mother has, in a peculiar degree, 'need of patience.' Heb. x. 36.

I. In trials of temper. 1 Cor. xiii. 4, 5, 7. Prov. xiv. 17.

II. With your children's faults.

Matt. xviii. 22, 35.

Look back to the days of your childhood.

Were not you equally trying to your mother?

Remember your own faults, and God's patience with you. He bears long with you.

III. It may be you need patience in bearing with unjust tempers, and unkind treatment. 1 Pet. ii. 19, 23. Ps. xxxvii. 7.

IV. For answers to prayer.

Syro-Phenician mother. Matt. xv. 22, 28. Jam. v. 7, 8. 'Tarry thou the Lord's leisure.'

V. In tribulation, sickness, and poverty. Rom. xii. 12. Jam. v. 10, 11. Luke, xxi. 19.

XIX.

THE FIRM MOTHER.

I. To obey is a child's duty.

    Exod. xx. 12. Eph. vi. 1. Col. iii. 20.

II. This obedience should be—

    1. Implicit.

    2. Unquestioning.

    3. Immediate.

    4. In manner, and spirit.

    5. From love.

    6. In absence, as well as presence.

    7. To the *mother* as well as the *father*.

        Prov. i. 8; vi. 20; xv. 20. Lev. xix. 3. *e.g.* Luke, ii. 51.

        This is most important. In the Bible no difference is drawn between the authority of the father and mother.

III. A promise attached to obedience.

    Exod. xx. 12. Eph. vi. 2. Jer. xxxv. 18, 19.

IV. To disobey is sin.

    Deut. xxi. 18, 21. Ezek. xxii. 7. Rom. i. 30. 2 Tim. iii. 2. 1 Sam. ii. 25.

V. A punishment attached to disobedience.

    Deut. xxvii. 16. Prov. xxx. 17.

VI. It is a parent's *duty* to enforce obedience. Allowed disobedience brings misery into the home. 1 Tim. iii. 4; v. 4.

    Eli. 1 Sam. ii. 23.

    David. 1 Kings, i. 6.

How solemn then, Mothers, is your responsibility.

How earnest should be your prayers that *your* commands may agree with God's. Gen. xviii. 19. Deut. xxxii. 46. Eph. vi. 1.

Seek for wisdom in commanding.

Firmness in insisting.

XX.

CONVERSION.

We meet time after time at our Mothers' Meeting, but how few of us are truly converted, and changed in heart.

Ask yourselves this night two questions.

I. Do you earnestly seek your own conversion? 'What shall it profit you, if you gain the whole world, and lose your own soul?'

Mark, viii. 36, 37.

Delay not. Isa. lix. 1.

II. Do you earnestly seek for the conversion of your children?

1. Perhaps you do not *care* for it. You do not seek *first* for them the kingdom of God. Matt. vi. 33. Be honest to yourselves in this matter. Are you ready to give up for them anything that keeps them from Christ?

   Matt. v. 29, 30.

2. Perhaps you do not *pray* for it.

   Observe how the mother prayed. Matt. xv. 22, 28. David. 1 Chron. xxix. 19. Job, i. 5.

3. Perhaps you place *hindrances* in the way.

   You draw them to the world instead of to Christ. Matt. xviii. 6.

4. Perhaps you forget the necessity of the *Holy Spirit's power*. Isa. xliv. 3, 4, 5.

   Pray this night for the outpouring of the Holy Spirit upon yourselves—your husbands—your children. Matt. vii. 11.

   Remember, 'except ye be converted, and become as little children, ye shall not enter into the kingdom of heaven.' Matt. xviii. 3.

XXI.

THOU, GOD, SEEST ME.

God's penetrating eye. Rev. i 14.

I. He sees *all*. Prov. v. 21.

    Bad and good. Prov. xv. 3.

II. *Where* does He see you?

    1. He sees the mother *in secret*. Matt. vi. 6.

        Each secret prayer—each sigh—each tear.

        No privacy from Him. Eccles. xii. 14. Ps. xix. 12. Jer. xxiii. 24.

        Many would give worlds to hide from God.

    2. In her *daily path*. Job, xxxiv. 21. Ps. cxxxix. 3.

    3. In *every circumstance*. 2 Chron. xvi. 9.

III. *What* does He see?

    1. The mother's *heart*. Jer. xx. 12. 1 Sam. xvi. 7. Her motives—desires—yearnings.

        You may deceive *others*. You may even deceive *yourselves*, 'but all things are naked, and opened unto the eyes of Him with whom we have to do.' Heb. iv. 13. Luke, xvi. 15.

    2. The mother's *sins*. Ps. xix. 12; xc. 8. Isa. lvii. 18. Amos, v. 12.

        Sins of omission and commission.

    3. The mother's *sorrows*. Exod. iii. 7.

        Both inward and outward trials. 2 Kings, xx. 5. Ps. cxlii. 3. Acts, vii. 34.

        There are many sorrows it is not well for a wife and mother to speak of to others, but take comfort! Your Saviour knows each grief—each trouble—each tear for your own sins or the sins of others.

    4. The mother's *need*. Matt. vi. 8, 32.

        And He promises to supply it. Ps. xxiii. 1. Philip, iv. 19.

XXII.

JESUS THE MOTHER'S FRIEND.

I. Mothers need a friend!

In joy and in sorrow, in dark hours and in light, in life and in death, they need a Friend who is always the same—even 'the same yesterday, to-day, and for ever.'

II. You may have such a Friend.

1. Even Jesus. Prov. xviii. 24. John, xv. 15. The Friend of sinners. Matt. xi. 19.

2. He loveth always. Prov. xvii. 17.

3. He is faithful. Prov. xviii. 24. John, xiii. 1.

III. Is He *your* Friend?

Can you point to Jesus and say, 'This is my Beloved, and this is my Friend?' Cant. v. 16.

If not, do not rest until you can say so.

IV. If Jesus *is* your Friend.

1. Go to Him in *trouble*. 'Pour out your heart before Him.' John, xi. 3, 11.

In sorrow lean on His bosom, as John did. John, xiii. 23.

'He weeps with those who weep.'

2. Go to Him in *joy*, for He 'rejoices with those who do rejoice.'

3. Do not have hard thoughts of Him because He afflicts.

'Faithful are the wounds of a friend.' Prov. xxvii. 6. Ps. cxli. 5.

He sympathises in every sorrow. Heb. iv. 15.

And has borne your griefs. Isa. liii. 4.

XXIII.

HELPS FOR MOTHERS.—PART I.

A mother has many hindrances in seeking Christ. She needs much help from the means of grace. To obtain this is often difficult, and requires much effort. Outward means are, therefore, too often neglected. If you would grow in grace this must not be.

Be diligent, therefore, in the use of—

I. Daily prayer. Matt. vi. 6, 11.

> No business should prevent this. David had the business of a kingdom upon him, nevertheless, he says, 'Evening, and morning, and at noon, will I pray.' Ps. lv. 17.

II. Daily Scripture reading. Acts, xvii. 11. Ps. cxix. 103.

III. Family prayer.

> Judgment pronounced on those who neglect family religion. Jer. x. 25.

> Promise to united prayer. Matt. xviii. 19, 20.

IV. Attendance on the public means of grace.

> Observe the command. Deut. xii. 12, 18. Heb. x. 25.

> What a blessing rested on it in the case of Lydia. Acts, xvi. 13, 15.

> There are great difficulties to the mother of a young family in going to Church on Sunday, but make an effort to overcome them. This can generally be done if husband and wife make a *united effort*.

> If you are truly hungering and thirsting after righteousness, you will earnestly use every means for obtaining the bread and the water of life. If you are careless in this respect, it is because there is no real hunger, no craving of soul for heavenly food.

XXIV.

HELPS FOR MOTHERS.—PART II.

We will notice this evening three more things which are, or ought to be, 'helps' to mothers on the heavenly race.

I. Husbands and wives should be *mutual* helps, (see Marriage Service) 'for the mutual help and comfort the one of the other.'

> Gen. ii. 18. 1 Pet. iii. 7. Eph. v. 28, 29.

> Fellow-pilgrims, fellow-sufferers, fellow-travellers they *must be*; but what an unspeakable joy is it when they are also fellow-helpers, fellow-labourers, fellow-heirs, fellow-citizens!

> 'O happy house, where man and wife are one,
> Thro' love of Thee, in spirit, heart, and mind;
> Together joined by holy bands, which none,
> Not death itself, can sever or unbind;
> Where both on thee unfailingly depend,
> In weal and woe, in good and evil days,
> And hope with Thee eternity to spend;
> In sweet communion and eternal praise.'

II. Christian friends.

> 2 Cor. i. 24. Rom. xvi. 3.

> What comfort and *help* may be derived from the visits, counsels, and sympathy of a Christian neighbour, a kind and devoted district visitor, or minister.

> Especially may Christian friends help each other by *prayer*. 2 Cor. i. 11. Jam. v. 16, 18. Matt. xviii. 19.

> How valuable is a Prayer Union, such as we have connected with our Mothers' Meeting.

III. But lastly remember that these 'helps' are worth nothing unless you have *the Lord for your Helper*. Ps. liv. 4. Heb. xiii. 6. Exod. xviii. 4.

> He is different to any earthly helper, for He is a Helper at all times, and in all circumstances.

> In trouble. Ps. xlvi. 1.

> To the widow. Ps. lxviii. 5.

To the fatherless. Ps. x. 14.

Take, therefore, this short prayer and use it in your daily life, 'Lord, be *Thou* my helper.' Lift up this prayer in the midst of your work—of temptation—of trial, and you will be enabled to add, 'My heart trusted in Him, and *I am helped*!' Ps. xxviii. 7.

XXV.

TEACH YOUR CHILDREN.

A mother may not have much time for instruction, or be very capable of teaching, but she should make it her daily duty to give her children some instruction in the Scriptures. She may know but little herself, but let not this discourage her; for in watering others she shall herself be watered. Prov. xi. 25.

I. Teach, seeking the help of the Holy Spirit. Isa. liv. 13. John, xvi. 13. Luke, xii. 12. Job, xxxvi. 22. Ps. xciv. 12.

II. Teach in the spirit of prayer.

Eph. vi. 18, 19.

Remembering these words, 'Without Me ye can do nothing.' John, xv. 5.

III. Teach, leaning on the promise.

Isa. lv. 10, 11. Eccles. xi. 1, 6.

IV. Teach, expecting a result.

Ps. cxxvi. 6. Prov. xxii. 6. Gen. xviii. 19. 2 Tim. i. 5; iii. 15.

XXVI.

THE PARTING PLACE, AND THE MEETING PLACE.

The following circumstance took place not long after the last meeting. Two mothers, who were both present at the Class, about a fortnight after met in the Cemetery, sorrowing at their children's graves. Each had during that interval lost a child, but not having heard of each other's trouble, the meeting was unexpected.

On this occasion the following subject was taken.

I. The parting place—the child's death-bed. This is,

    1. A parting place.

        All must die alone. The mother may have watched over her child with untiring care during its years of infancy, the trials of youth, and the snares and cares of riper years, but here they *must part*. 2 Sam. xii. 15, 23.

    2. A weeping place. Gen. xxi. 16.

        2 Sam. xii. 21. Jer. xxxi. 15.

        Mark, v. 38. Luke, vii. 13. Not *wrong*, for Jesus wept at the grave of Lazarus. John, xi. 35.

    3. A birth place

        To a new and heavenly life. But not so to *all*. To *some*, namely, to those who have indeed been born again. Luke, xvi. 22; and to babes. Isa. xl. 11.

        Contrast David's sorrow for his infant, (2 Sam. xii. 23) with his sorrow for Absalom, 2 Sam. xix. 4. To one death was the door of *life*, to the other of *death*.

II. The meeting place—the judgment-seat. Rev. xx. 12. Rom. xiv. 10.

    You cannot avoid it.

    It will be.

    1. To all a place of recognition.

        The child you led to Christ—the child you led astray. The child you trained for heaven—the child you trained for hell. *All* will be there.

    2. To many a place of weeping. Matt. xxv. 30. Luke, vi. 25.

3. To many a place of rejoicing. Matt. xxv. 34.

Believing mother! Your night of weeping will then be over, your morning of joy will dawn, of which the sun will never set! Ps. xxx. 5.

Which will it be to you—a meeting-place of joy or sorrow?

May you and your children be so united in Christ here, that you may both part and meet in peace!

XXVII.

THE MOTHER'S DEATH-BED.

On the occasion of the death of a young mother, which took place not long after the first meeting in the new year.

I. How near it may be. 1 Sam. xx. 3. Job, xxi. 13.

> In the midst of life we are in death.
>
> We have had a solemn lesson. Almost the youngest in our class cut down the first.

II. The hour of death is an hour

> 1. Of deep solemnity.
>
> > It is a dark valley. Ps. xxiii. 4. Job. x. 21.
>
> 2. Of much regret.
>
> > Conscience awake, looks back on duties undone—things done—words spoken—words unsaid, &c.
>
> 3. Often of great suffering. Ps. cxvi. 3.
>
> > Not the time to begin to seek the Lord.
>
> 4. Of parting. Philip, i. 23, 24.
>
> > Must die alone. Must leave husband and children. They may go with you to the edge of the river, but no further.
>
> 5. Of weeping. Gen. xxxv. 18; xxiii. 2. John, xi. 31. 2 Sam. xix. 4.
>
> 6. It is an hour when Christ, and *Christ alone*, can save you.
>
> > Thus we pray, 'In the hour of death, and in the day of judgment, Good Lord, deliver us.'
> >
> > His rod and staff alone can help you. Ps. xxiii. 4.
> >
> > He alone can take away the sting from death. 1 Cor. xv. 55, 57. Rom. viii. 38, 39. Isa. xliii. 2.
> >
> > It is only if washed in His blood, and clothed in His righteousness, that you need not fear to appear before God.

XXVIII.

NEW YEAR'S DAY.

'I must work the work of Him that sent me while it is day: the night cometh, when no man can work.'—John, ix. 4.

Time *past*—is gone, thou canst not it recall.
Time *is*—thou hast, improve the portion small.
Time *future*—is not, and may never be.
Time *present*—is the only time for thee!

Therefore,

I. *Hear to-day.* (Ps. xcv. 7.) 'See that ye refuse not Him that speaketh.'

Exhort to-day your children. (Heb. iii. 13.)

Work to-day (John, ix. 4) for your children's souls.

Never postpone. Jam. iv. 13. 2 Cor. vi. 2.

Now it is high time to wake out of sleep. Rom. xiii. 11.

II. Because the *night* cometh when no man can work. John, ix. 4.

The night of *your* death—your *husband's* death—your *children's* death.

Perhaps this sentence has gone forth against you, or yours, 'This year thou shalt die.' Jer. xxviii. 16.

Luke, xii. 20; xiii. 7.

Mothers, *awake!* to your own, and your children's danger.

Awake to the importance of safety in Christ.

Mothers, *work!* for yourselves, for your families.

'Labour not for the meat which perisheth, but for that meat which endureth unto everlasting life.' John, vi. 27.

XXIX.

FIRST MEETING IN THE YEAR.

I. Look backwards on the past year.

  1. On your *sins*.

    They are many—great—mighty. You need forgiveness, and Christ is *ready* to forgive. Neh. ix. 17. Make this your prayer for the past year, 'Lord, pardon mine iniquity, for *it is great.*' Ps. xxv. 11.

    On your sins towards your *husbands*. Provocation—temper—carelessness of their comfort—an unyielding spirit. Again must you say, 'Pardon mine iniquity, for it is *great.*'

    On your sins towards your *children*. Neglect—bad example—prayerlessness—cross tempers—hasty slaps. Again you must say, 'Pardon mine iniquity, for it is *great.*'

  2. On your *sorrows*.

    Poverty—sickness—death. Yet your sorrows not so many as your sins. How have you been helped through them! Have you *profited*? Heb. xii. 10. God has been teaching you, have you learnt the lesson?

  3. On your mercies.

    You can count your sorrows. Try and count your mercies, they are more than can be numbered. Ps. xl. 5. How undeserved they were! You have counted your days of sickness—have you those of health? Your hours of mourning—have you those of joy? Your children taken—have you counted your children spared? &c., &c. Were you thankful? Gen. xxxii. 10.

II. Look forward on the opening year.

  On what? Can you tell?

  How uncertain, you know not what will be even on the morrow. Jam. iv. 4. Prov. xxvii. 1. Who will be taken? Whose husband? Whose child?

  You know not.

  Therefore, 'be ye also ready, for in such an hour as ye *think not* the Son of Man cometh.' Matt. xxiv. 44.

  Can *you* say, 'Even so come, Lord Jesus, *come quickly*?'

XXX.

LAST MEETING IN THE YEAR.
THE CRADLE AND THE GRAVE.

God has been speaking to us during the past year. Two mothers have gone to their long home, and ten of our children. Let us reply, 'Speak, Lord, for thy servant heareth.' 1 Sam. iii. 9.

God speaks to us from the cradle, and the grave.

I. From the *cradle*, and says,

    1. 'Take this child, and nurse it for *me*.' Exod. ii. 9.

    2. Pray for it—train it—love it—comfort it.

    3. He speaks in a voice of *comfort* from our cradles to our souls, if we are His people. 'Mother, can you forget this sucking child? Yea, you *may* forget, yet will not I forget you.' Isa. xlix. 15.

        Again—Do you comfort your babe—do you soothe its fears? do you wipe its tears? Even so, believing mother, will God comfort you. Isa. lxvi. 13. Yes, even 'wipe away all tears from your eyes.'

    Oh! precious voice from the cradle to your soul!

II. God speaks from the *grave*—and says,

    1. 'Give an account of thy stewardship, for thou mayst be no longer steward.' Luke, xvi. 2.

    2. 'Time is short.'

        1 Cor. vii. 29. 1 Pet. iv. 7.

        What a little life—gone as a spark!

        You may die—your children may die—or Christ may come. Do not say, 'to-morrow.' Jam. iv. 13.

    3. 'Be ye also ready.'

        Matt. xxiv. 44.

    4. Your child shall rise again.

        'I am the resurrection and the life.' John, xi. 25. (See Burial Service.) Jer. xxxi. 16, 17.

If both parent and child are in Christ, what a blessed reunion, for He adds, 'Whosoever liveth and believeth in me shall *never die!'*

If it should be the Lord's will during the coming year again to take many of our little ones from their mothers' arms, and to lay them in His own bosom, may each sorrowing one amongst us be enabled to say in the spirit of true and loving submission, 'The Lord gave, and the Lord hath taken away; *blessed be the name of the Lord!'*

Lector House believes that a society develops through a two-fold approach of continuous learning and adaptation, which is derived from the study of classic literary works spread across the historic timeline of literature records. Therefore, we aim at reviving, repairing and redeveloping all those inaccessible or damaged but historically as well as culturally important literature across subjects so that the future generations may have an opportunity to study and learn from past works to embark upon a journey of creating a better future.

This book is a result of an effort made by Lector House towards making a contribution to the preservation and repair of original ancient works which might hold historical significance to the approach of continuous learning across subjects.

HAPPY READING & LEARNING!

LECTOR HOUSE LLP
E-MAIL: lectorpublishing@gmail.com

www.ingramcontent.com/pod-product-compliance
Lightning Source LLC
Chambersburg PA
CBHW030415160726
47992CB00007B/3135